YOUR YES WILL COST

You

30 DAY JOURNAL
EMBRACING THE YEAR OF YES

SHAJUANA R DITTO

INTRODUCTION

HELLO MY BEAUTIFUL FRIENDS!
AS YOU ALL KNOW, WE SAY YES
TO VARIOUS COMMITMENTS AND
ACTIVITIES ON THE DAILY. FROM
WORK AND SOCIAL
OBLIGATIONS, FAMILY
RESPONSIBILITIES, PERSONAL
DEVELOPMENT AND OFFERING
OUR TIME AND SKILLS; WHAT WE
SAY YES TO REFLECTS OUR
PRIORITIES AND SHAPES OUR
LIVES. IN THE NEXT THIRTY DAYS,
MY PRAYER IS THAT YOU BECOME
MINDFUL OF WHAT YOU ARE
GIVING YOUR ATTENTION TO AND
HOW THAT IS SHAPING YOUR
FAITH.IF NOTHING ELSE, MY
SINCERE PRAYER IS THAT
THROUGHOUT THE PAGES, I HOPE
THIS DEVOTIONAL IGNITES YOUR
EXCITEMENT FOR READING THE
WORD OF GOD AND DEEPENS
YOUR RELATIONSHIPS WITH HIM.
YOUR YES WILL COST
you

YOUR
YES
WILL
COST
YOU

30 DEVOTIONS TO NURTURE YOUR SPIRITUAL GROWTH. EMBRACING A
TRANSFORMATIVE PATH THAT WILL IGNITE YOUR EXCITEMENT
FOR READING THE WORD OF GOD. EACH PAGE OF THIS INTERACTIVE
DEVOTION IS UNIQUE, JUST LIKE OUR DAYS. IT IS DESIGNED TO INSPIRE,
ENGAGE AND EQUIP YOU ON YOUR PERSONAL JOURNEY.

CONTENTS

CONTENTS

MONDAY
Day 1

PRAY   Plan   Prepare

PSALM 4:5 MSG

WAIT EXPECTANTLY...

Expectation is the
birthing ground for
a miracle
@Pastor Sheryl Brady

In a world filled with hurried impatience, there is wisdom found in Psalm 4:5. This scripture uncovers the beauty of aligning our hearts with God's timing. As we embark on this collective journey, we find ourselves in a perpetual state of anticipation of the next significant moment or the hope for a positive turnaround, we are all waiting for. Expectation, may be the contributing factor of if you move forward or stay stuck. Navigating the path of expectation, we call upon Jesus to strengthen our faith, recognizing that waiting expectantly on the Lord is the key to unveiling our next steps. If you are needing a miracle in your life, you must command your soul to expect.

As we wait expectantly, acknowledging God's sovereignty over our lives and trusting in the Lord are pre-requisites of the sacrifice of our wait. Saying yes to God involves us surrendering our timelines and embracing His perfect timing. Waiting expectantly signifies an active trust, knowing that God's plans are far greater than our own. Do you trust God's unfolding plan? Are you being patient through the process? As you are waiting expectantly, God is producing and transforming our resilient nature to depend on Him. Waiting expectantly deepens our relationship with Him. Wait on the Lord so that He may renew your strength.

Saying Yes to God's
plan empowers us to
walk boldly.
When we say yes to God, we
align ourselves with
His promises, we embrace
His truth and we walk in the
confidence that comes from
Christ. Walk in "God-fidence"
today! This is not the season to
get ahead of God.

NOTES

Pray

My Personal Prayer:

My Daily Decree: Today,
I DECREE...

TUESDAY

Day

PRAY   Plan   Prepare

COLOSSIANS 3:9 MSG

YOUR YES NEEDS
YOU TO FOCUS ON
YOUR FRONT ROW

Recently, I heard a speaker say these words: "Focus on the people who will sit front row at your funeral." Saying YES to God intricately connects with saying yes to His people. When saying YES there is a significance of staying focused on the right people and cultivating healthy relationships in the context of our faith. When we say yes to God, our faith journey is interwoven with relationships. Consider who will sit front row at your funeral- those who have shared in our joys and sorrows, those who have seen your faith in action. Saying yes to God is an affirmation of love that involves saying yes to His people.

In Colossians 3:9 we are putting off the old self: in this verse, Paul urges the Colossians to shed their old selves, emphasizing the transformative power of Christ. Saying yes to God involves a continual process of aligning ourselves with His truth and shedding the negativity that hinders our spiritual growth. We need to identify those who encourage us, see us, provide a safe space for us. We don't have to like everyone but we are commanded to love everyone. The world may bombard us with negative opinions, casting doubt on our worth and purpose, as a follower of Christ, but our confidence is rooted in Him.

Saying yes to God, means your wait is marked with expectancy. We must know that His timing orchestrates beautiful outcomes. You are marked for the moment and the movement.

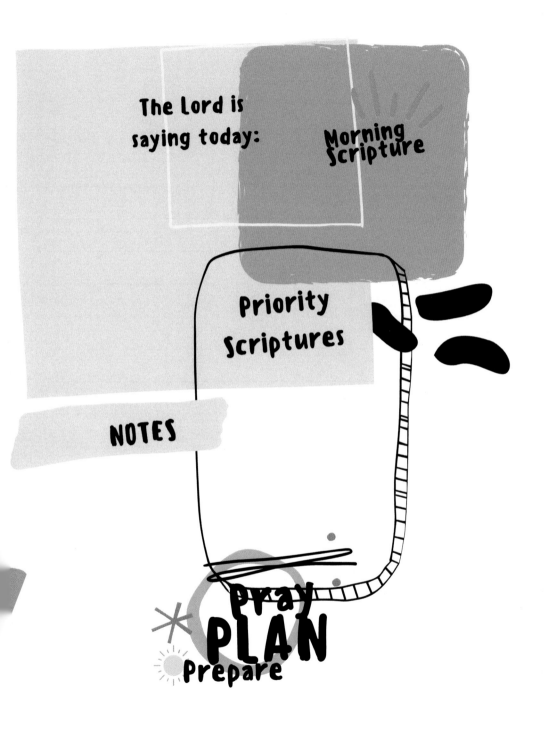

The Lord is
saying today:

Morning
Scripture

Priority
Scriptures

NOTES

Pray
PLAN
Prepare

NOTES

Pray

My Personal Prayer:

My Daily Decree: Today, I DECREE...

WEDNESDAY
Day

PRAY   Plan   Prepare

PSALM 24 MSG

WAKE UP!
Wake Up!
Wake Up!

I have the awesome privilege of serving at this amazing ministry called: Upper Room. I remember when I heard the spirit of the Lord prompting His people to: Wake up!Wake up! Wake up! In Psalm 24, we find an invitation to recognize the importance of our spiritual awakening. There must be a mindful connection that speaks to our core on the daily. God desires our attentiveness. He calls us to be vigilant and receptive to His word, His will and His wonder. There must be an intentional commitment to God's truth and a surrender to His divine plan. Psalm 24 in the year 2024 is paramount in this season. Not sure what to pray for? Pray Psalm 24 over your day.

Psalm 24:7-8 says "Wake up, you sleepyhead city! Wake up, you sleepyhead people! The King of Glory is ready to enter," if you have time today, please read this scripture! Today, you can not become dormant. You can not be distracted by routines and a mediocre spirit. We must be intentional about meeting with God and waiting on Him to enter into our sacred spaces. We must make an intentional choice to be attentive to His word. Psalm 24 is a call to have clean hands and a pure heart. In this season you must shake off the slumber of being stagnant, and complacent. You must be vigilant in seeking Him and His guidance. Wake up! Wake up! Wake up!

Our yes is a dynamic force waiting to be activated. Our Psalm 24 'yes' acknowledges and embraces a stirring for clean hands and a pure heart. We must wake up to the call that resonates within us. Will you say yes in asking God to create in you a clean heart and renew a right spirit within you?May our prayer today be: Lord prepare me to be a sanctuary, pure and holy tried and true. And with thanksgiving I'll be a living Sanctuary for You.

NOTES

The Lord is
saying today:

Morning
Scripture

Priority
Scriptures

NOTES

Pray
PLAN
Prepare

THURSDAY

Day

PRAY   Plan   Prepare

ROMANS 8:8 MSG

YOUR YES WILL DEMAND YOU TO REBUKE YOUR FLESH

There is a constant battle between our fleshly desires and our commitment to faith. As Romans 8:8 reminds us, those who are in the flesh cannot please God. It is a daily challenge to prioritize our faith over our fleeting desires. Romans 7:18-19 we find internal conflict. We must understand and acknowledge our human tendency to be led by the flesh. We must be vigiliant in our daily choices. Our commitment to faith should supersede the desires of the flesh. Remember Romans 8:8 and the call to please God in all we do.

Today, be reminded, it is through: prayer, discipline and the renewing of your mind that will help make faith decisions instead of fleshly decisions. We are constantly in a a war between our flesh and our spirit. Before your feet hit the ground, you must let the atmosphere know that you are going to make choices that please God. Dear Friend, there will always be a battle within. But, remember that James 4:7-8 has two strategies: submit to God and resist the enemy. When your negative attitude rises up today, submit to God and resist the enemy. When your mind falls back into old thinking patterns, submit to God and resist the enemy.

Win the battle within
by submitting and
resisting your carnal
and fleshly desires.
Your yes is making a
commitment to submit
to God and resist the
schemes of the enemy.
In the choices that you
make today, allow your
faith to triumph over
your flesh. Say yes to
rebuking your flesh.

The Lord is
saying today:

Morning
Scripture

Priority
Scriptures

NOTES

Pray
PLAN
Prepare

NOTES

Pray
PLAN
Prepare

My Personal Prayer:

My Daily Decree:
Today,
I DECREE...

FRIDAY
Day

PRAY   Plan   Prepare

1 CORINTHIANS 15:58 ESV

HOLD THE LINE

2024 I specifically heard the spirit of the Lord say:"Hold the Line!"Although this is my word for the year, I want to share how it resonates with 1 Corinthians 15:58, reminding us that we must be steadfast in the Lord. "Holding the Line" emphasizes the call to be steadfast and immovable. We must stand firm in our walk with Christ and trust in God despite challenges we may face. As we trust God and hold Him to His word, may we experience breakthrough and healing in our lives and in our families lives. This rollercoaster type of Christianity must come to a halt in this season. God is calling us to a higher level of consistency.

This prompt to "Hold the Line," demands a certain posture of heart. As we hold the line for our friends, may we have the faith to speak to their situations and circumstances and things begin to change in their lives. As we hold the line for our community may we persevere in the face of competition and difficulties. As we hold the line for our families, let us anticipate breakthrough that leads to miraculous encounters that only we could cultivate by the Holy Spirit. As we hold the line for ourselves, may healing take place in our minds and our souls. Keep holding the line this year even when you are at the end of the rope.

Say this out loud with me this morning:
As I hold the line for: my friends, my family and my community; I am saying yes to being steadfast. I commit to hold the line in faith. As I hold the line, I declare that I am one step closer to breakthrough. I am one step closer to healing. I am one step closer to glory. I am one step closer to not being moved. My yes to standing firm allows breakthrough, miracles, healing and blessings to find me as I give myself fully to the work of the Lord.

The Lord is
saying today:

Morning
Scripture

Priority
Scriptures

NOTES

Pray
PLAN
Prepare

NOTES

SATURDAY
Day

6

PRAY   Plan   Prepare

PSALM 91:1-2 ESV

YOUR YES WILL NEED
YOU TO GIVE
YOURSELF PERMISSION
TO REST

Good Morning Sweet Friend,
One thing I want you to focus on
this morning is the word abide. To
abide means to: accept, endure, or
tolerate. This is the
encouragement for the day: today,
you can find security and refuge in
His presence. John 15:4 says,"Abide
in me, and I in you." Whatever you
may be facing today, please know:
God is beside you, He has gone
before you and He lives in you.
When you are feeling overwhelmed
remember Isaiah 26:3. It's okay to
slow down and give yourself
permission to rest in His presence.
Psalm 46:1 says that God is our
refuge and strength, a very
present help in trouble.

If your spirit if feeling troubled today, ask the Lord to help you abide in Him. I want to ask you to consider what obstacles or distractions that are hindering you from abiding in God's presence? What does it mean to you to abide in His presence? As we say 'yes' to God; our willingness to abide in His shelter leads to a life that is anchored in Him. As we open up our hearts in the next few days and ask the Lord for transforming power, seeking God's shelter brings assurance and protection. I believe as David was writing Psalm 91, He was reminding himself that their is protection and security in the dwelling space of our Savior.

Saying yes
to God grants
me a sense
of peace and rest.

The Lord is
saying today:

Morning
Scripture

Priority
Scriptures

NOTES

Pray

PLAN

Prepare

Pray

My Personal Prayer:

My Daily Decree: Today, I DECREE...

SUNDAY
Day 1

PRAY   Plan   Prepare

PROVERBS 10:17
MSG
NEW SEASONS REQUIRE NEW DISCIPLINES

"The road to life is a disciplined life: ignore correction and you're lost for good." As you and I reflect on this passage from Proverbs 10:17, my prayer today is that we are intentional about spiritual disciplines. The way to a fulfilled life means we embrace a life of correction. Everyone that keeps you accountable is not always attacking you. Resisting correction will have a huge impact on your spiritual, emotional, and relational well-being. Proverbs 12:1 says, "Whoever loves discipline loves knowledge, but he who hates reproof is stupid." Proverbs 19:20(NIV): "Listen to advice and accept discipline, and at the end you be counted among the wise." I tell my friends all the time, "Don't sit in your stuck."

The "don't sit in your stuck," phrase is the mentality of not allowing your circumstance to send you into a down hill spiral. Have your moment, but then have a Talitha Koum spirit. Talitha Koum is a phrase spoken by Jesus in Mark 5:41 that translates into "Little girl, I say to you, get up." Where ever you are in your life right now: Talitha Koum (GET UP!) Living a disciplined life enables you to concentrate on challenges, situations, and circumstances, fostering moments akin to "Talitha Koum," where you get up with renewed strength. Your 'yes' today says: Get up out of your negative mentality. Get up out of that pit of darkness! Get up and say YES to the promises of God. New seasons require new disciplines.

NOTES

Pray

My Personal Prayer:

My Daily Decree: Today, I DECREE...

MONDAY
Day

8

PRAY   Plan   Prepare

1 Peter 5:8 ESV

DISTRACTIONS WILL ALWAYS DELAY YOUR DESTINY

It is Day 8 friends. The number 8 is often associated with new beginnings. Maybe today, is your new beginning. I want to start with a question: "What are common distractions in your daily life that hinder your spiritual focus?" Go ahead and write those down. Take a moment to pause for a moment and ask Holy Spirit to reveal to you what has you most distracted this month. One example from the Bible where distractions led to delays is the story of Jonah. In the book of Jonah, God instructs Jonah to go to the city of Nineveh and deliver a message of repentance. Jonah becomes distacted by his own fears and prejuidces, attempting to flee from God's command by boarding a ship heading in the opposite direction.

Have you ever gone in the opposite direction that God specifically told you to go? Jonah story illustrates how distractions, in this case driven by fear and personal biases, can lead to delays in fulfilling God's intended purpose. 2009, the Lord dropped this word down in my lap: "Distractions will delay your destiny." We must align our 'yes' to God with intentional focus, avoiding unnecessary diversions. Matthew 26:41 ESV "Watch and pray that you may not enter into temptation. The spirit indeed is willing, but the flesh is weak." Ask Holy Spirit today to help you recognize your weaknesses. Despite our good intentions, there will always be a battle between your spirit and your flesh.

To avoid distractions this month, be aware of Jesus' instruction to watch and pray. I want to encourage you with a lifestyle of vigilance and communion with God to navigate challenges. As we surrender our weaknesses to God, be encouraged to seek His strength to overcome any and all distractions. Remember, that in our weakness, God's strength is made perfect. (2 Corinthians 12:9.) During your prayer time today, rely on the Holy Spirit to navigate challenges and distractions. Also, pray that His power will be made perfect in your weakness. As distractions come this month, allow your 'yes' to focus on your divine destiny.

PLAN

The Lord is
saying today:

Morning
Scripture

Priority
Scriptures

Pray
PLAN
Prepare

NOTES

TUESDAY
Day

PRAY   Plan   Prepare

2 Peter 3:18 ESV

YOUR YES NEEDS
YOU TO GROW
THROUGH WHAT
YOU GO THROUGH

2 Peter 3:18 "But grow in the grace and knowledge of our Lord and Savior Jesus Christ."Growth involves a process. If I was standing in a pulpit right now, this is what I would say: "Turn and tell your neighbor, I must GROW through what I GO through." Although life often presents challenges, there is an opportunity for growth. The scripture encourages us to grow in the grace and knowledge of Jesus Christ. Two words to focus on today: Grace and Knowledge. Please understand that just because you are challenged doesn't mean you are not chosen. You are still Chosen. You are still a royal priesthood. You can move forward. Again, pray for grace and knowledge specifically today.

Deepening your knowledge of Jesus Christ involves a multifaceted approach that encompasses discipline. Spiritual disciplines refer to: studying the bible, prayer, worship and growing daily in your relationship with Him. If you find yourself in a season of complacency or stagnation, it's an indication that personal growth is not occurring. At the end of this specific verse, it concludes with "Amen." "Amen," means "let it be so." When you and I say "Amen," we are in agreement with Heaven and the word of God. Remember that God's promises are 'Yes' and amen as it reads in 2 Corinthians 1:20. Today, allow your 'yes' to grow in grace and knowledge.

NOTES

The Lord is
saying today:

Morning
Scripture

Priority
Scriptures

NOTES

pray
PLAN
Prepare

WEDNESDAY

Day 10

PRAY   Plan   Prepare

GENESIS 24 NIV

PRAY SPECIFICALLY AND THE LORD WILL ANSWER INTENTIONALLY

Today and Tomorrow will be your first Faith excerise days. Today, read Genesis 24 carefully and in a quiet place. Use the space provided to write specifically what you are praying for.

The Lord is
saying today:

Morning
Scripture

Priority
Scriptures

Pray
PLAN
Prepare

NOTES

THURSDAY

Day

11

PRAY   Plan   Prepare

ROMANS 12:1 NIV

YOUR YES WON'T ALLOW YOU TO PLAY IT SAFE

Saying yes to God, requires you to be uncomfortable. Playing it safe all the time will only get you so far on your journey. "Faith without works is dead,"James 2:17. You must put your FAITH to work by believing what the word of God says. Your declaration for today needs to be: "If God said it, I believe it and that settles it." Your Yes needs you to take the risk.

Faith Exercise Day!

Today, focus on marked moments. Marked Moments are created when you are present in every moment of your life. Around this clock, plan out your day. As you plan out your day, ask the Lord to allow you to BE where your feet are. Ask Him to reveal miracles that need to be seen.

FRIDAY
Day 12

PRAY   Plan   Prepare

The words of Isaiah 1:17 urges us to "Learn to do good;" These words are action words that guide us to live a life marked by righteousness, justice and compassion. "Learn to do good." There must be intentional effort to understand that we need goodness in our thoughts, words and actions. How can I grow in goodness? Galatians 5:22-23 lists the fruits of the Spirit, including love, joy, peace, patience, kindness, goodness, faithfulness, gentleness, and self control. Through the Holy Spirit's work in our life, we must strive to cultivate and develop these fruits in our everyday lives. Hebrews 13:16 reminds us to not neglect to do good and to share what we have, for such sacrifices are pleasing to God.

We should strive to do good to others not to seek God's approval or rewards. Instead, it should flow naturally from the genuine care and compassion that stems from the mature and developed spiritual fruit evident in our lives. The power of 'yes' to good works should be an affirmation of love and kindness. "God-winks," are those unexpected, divine moments of grace over your life. Today, allow the God who lives inside of you bring out the goodness through you. Do the right thing, not because you're expecting anything but because He's given you everything.

The Lord is
saying today:

Morning
Scripture

Priority
Scriptures

NOTES

Pray
PLAN
Prepare

My Personal Prayer:

My Daily Decree: Today,
I DECREE...

Pray
PLAN
Prepare

SATURDAY

Day 13

PRAY   Plan   Prepare

2 Cor. 10:3-5 ESV

Your YES will require you to stop rehearsing negative thoughts that are lies from the pits of hell

There is so much wisdom in 2 Corinthians 10:3-5. Do me a favor, write or underline words in this scripture that stick out to you. The scripture teaches us about the power of our thoughts and the importance of rehearsing negative patterns in our minds. I encourage you, for further reading, please go get: <u>The Power to Change</u> by Pastor Craig Groescel. 2 Corinthians 10:3-5 is one of those authortaive scriptures that you can walk around your house when the enemy is messing with your mind. This is the scriptures you just begin to declare out loud. I destroy arguments and every lofty opinion rising against the knowledge of God and take every thought captive to obey Christ. Apostle Paul reminds us that the true battleground is not physical but within the realm of our thoughts. If we are not careful, negative thoughts can become strongholds, influencing our emotions, actions and ultimately, our spiritual well-being. How do you dismantle strongholds and negative thought patters that hinder your walk with God? Through prayer, reading the word and reliance on the Holy Spirit. We have the power and the authority over negative thoughts that enter into our minds. Taking every thought captive must be an ongoing practice as you say 'yes' to the things of God. Dismantling strongholds is an active and intentional process. We must submit our minds to His authority, invite His truth to reshape our perspectives and commit to surrender our thoughts to Him. Romans 12:2 reminds us to renew our minds. Negative thoughts, unbelieving thoughts, lustful thoughts, prideful thoughts, racing thoughts, we speak to you now and we say "submit to His word, right now!" We must stop entertaining these thoughts and allowing them to grip our hearts. Breaking the cycle of rehearsing negative thoughts needs a mindset grounded in faith and trust in God. Our thought life plays a significant role with our relationship with Christ. We must wage war daily against any negative thoughts. I declare war over my thoughts and receive God's truth today.

NOTES

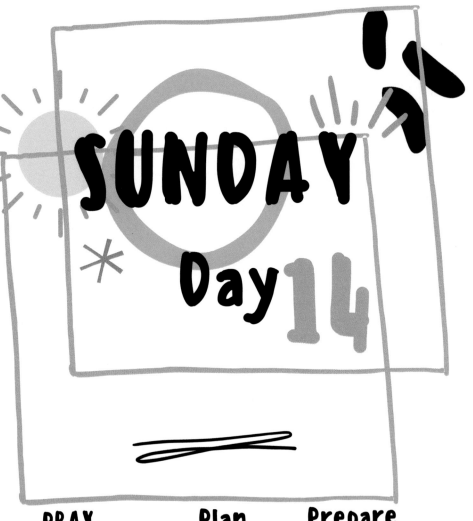

SUNDAY

Day 14

PRAY   Plan   Prepare

GENESIS 18:14 ESV

WHEN YOU
CAN'T
REMEMBER
HE CAN

Genesis 18:14 "Is anything too hard for the Lord?" Today, there is a powerful assurance found in the word of God. When we find ourselves in situations where we can't see the way forward, we must remember the limitless power of His love. Whatever your situation may be right now, please understand that there is nothing too challenging, too complex, or impossible for Him. If you don't put a limit on God, He will not put a limit on you. Maybe you are feeling overwhelmed as you are reading today. Maybe you have lost sight of the One who can overcome any obstacle. Let me remind you, when you can't remember: He Can! God has proven Himself to be trustworthy, reliable and capable of the miraculous. When you and I remember Philippians 4:13 that we can do all things through Christ who strengthens us: we come into agreement that there is noting too hard for the Lord. Remembering that there is nothing too hard for the Lord should be a daily reminder that our abilities are not limited to our own strength. Our faith must be anchored in the limitless strength of Christ working within us. Let me remind you over and over again: that nothing is too hard for the Lord. As strength rises today:walk in the confidence of Christ, knowing that He who has been faithful in the past will remain faithful in every situation.

The Lord is
saying today:

Morning
Scripture

Priority
Scriptures

NOTES

Pray
PLAN
Prepare

NOTES

Pray

My Personal Prayer:

My Daily Decree:
Today, I DECREE...

Pray
PLAN
Prepare

MONDAY
Day 15

PRAY   Plan   Prepare

2 PETER 3:9 ESV

YOUR YES WILL
BRING YOU: PAIN,
PEACE and PURPOSE
DEPENDING ON THE
SEASON

2 Peter 3:9; Romans 8:28; Philippians 4:7 will be your focus scriptures for today. Write them on your bathroom mirror, your prayer wall or on your palm as a friendly reminder for today. In this season, seek the peace that surpasses understanding. God's peace is a constant companion even in uncertain situations. Although you may be facing challenges this season, they are just opportunities for God to work for your good. Trust that even in pain, His purpose is at play shaping and molding you for His divine plan. I want to encourage you today that "the Lord is not slow to fulfill his promises as some count as slowness, but is patient toward you, not wishing that any should perish,

but that should reach repentance."
The Lord is inviting us to a life of
repentance and the hopeful promise
of salvation. Peter addresses God's
timing as "apparent slowness." God's
"slowness" is not a delay but rather
an expression of His patience and
protection. Remember that every
delay does not mean that you have
been denied by God. Every delay does
not mean that God is mad at you.
Please remember that God operates
outside of our timetable. As we say
'yes' to purpose we are saying "yes"
to the divine and direct timing of
God. We are also saying 'yes' to His
promises being fulfilled in our life.
We are partnering with God for His
plan and invited to partner with Him
in His redemptive purpose.

NOTES

TUESDAY
Day

16

PRAY   Plan   Prepare

LUKE 6:46 ESV

THE LORD IS
NOT OBLIGATED
TO REPEAT
HIMSELF TWICE

I want you to remember a time when your parents asked you do the simplest of tasks like cleaning your room. Remember your mom's tone when she asked you the first time. Now, remember her tone the third time she asked. Not only her tone, remember when she said your full name so that you would know the seriousness of the situation. Today, our focus is cultivating a responsive heart through prayer. God is not obligated to repeat himself twice. James 1:22 is a friendly reminder that we must be doers of the word, and not hearers only, deceiving ourselves. Luke 6:46 says, "Why do you call me 'Lord, Lord',and do not do what I tell you? This verse is highlighting the importance of aligning our actions with our faith. When you and I call ourselves Disciples it involves obedience in following the teachings and principles laid out by Jesus Christ. The Lord doesn't have to say my full name to get me to do what He asked me to do. Remember delayed obedience is still disobedience. Obedience in discipleship is about aligning our actions with the teachings of Jesus and growing in our faith through a commitment to live according to his example. Luke 11:28 "But he said, 'Blessed rather are those who hear the word of God and keep it.' Again, our focus today is hearing the word of the Lord and actively living according to His command. What challenges or obstacles do you face in promptly obeying God's voice in your life? If you remember in Genesis 12:1-4 Abraham was called to leave his country and go to a land that the Lord would show him. Because of Abraham's obedience, God established a covenant with Abraham promising to bless him and make his descendants into a great nation. Our obedience could be tied to generational blessings. Your 'yes' may not be just for you, but for your family and the people around you. When the Lord speaks, we must move. We must move even when the path seems uncertain. We must listen when we may struggle to recognize God's guidance. When we say 'yes' to God's plans, we must move promptly and obediently.

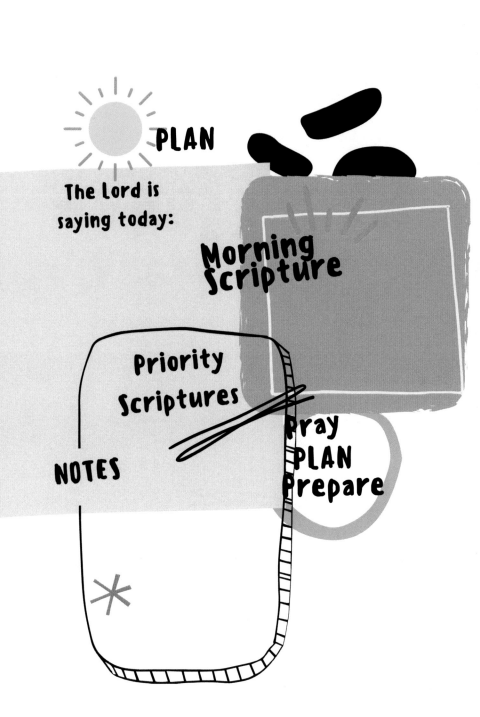

PLAN

The Lord is
saying today:

Morning
Scripture

Priority
Scriptures

Pray
PLAN
Prepare

NOTES

WEDNESDAY
Day 11

PRAY   Plan   Prepare

LUKE 14:16:22 ESV

YOUR YES MUST INVITE JESUS INTO ALL OF YOUR PLANS

You are invited! Luke 14:16 encourages us to invite Jesus into all aspects of our lives, which includes all of our plans and endeavors. Imagine with me being invited to the most elaborate dinner party that Jesus has ever prepared. Now, imagine making an excuse of why you couldn't attend. That's what we do right? We make excuses all the time when the Lord has invited us to commune with Him. Our quiet time is the banquet. Sunday mornings in corporate worship is an invitation to sit at his feet. This parable in Luke 14:16 illustrates the urgency of responding to the invitation to the kingdom of God. The excuses given in this scripture given by the guests reflect the distractions that can hinder our willingness to embrace

God's plan for our lives. God desires a full house- a life overflowing with His presence and purpose. We can not prioritize our plans over God's calling. When we do make excuses, we risk missing out on the abundant blessings and fulfillment that comes from aligning our lives with His will. What's the strategy to invite Him into all of our plans? We must: acknowledge His sovereignty, seek His guidance and we must be open to redirection. Have you invited Jesus into every aspect of your plans? Are you, like the guests in the parable, making excuses based on worldly pursuits and distractions? Today, respond by recognizing that you have been invited to sit and dine at His table.

By inviting God into every detail, we transform the ordinary into the extraordinary. With our hearts open and a 'yes' on our lips; Let us discover that His presence is the truest joy, and His guidance is the compass that leads us to a life beyond our wildest dreams. We must align our plans with God's purpose. You and I must surrender our desires and trust in His perfect plan for our lives.

THURSDAY
Day
18

PRAY   Plan   Prepare

STOP MATCHING ENERGY and START SHIFTING ATMOSPHERES

In 2 Chronicles 15, we witness a significant moment where the people of Israel recognize the need for a divine shift. The atmosphere shifted as their commitment echoed with loud acclamation, shouting, and the resounding sound of trumpets and horns. You and I have the power to shift any atmosphere that we walk in. In the context of 2 Chronicles 15:13-14, taking an oath to the Lord with loud acclamation, shouting, and with trumpets and horns signifies a deeply, commitment to seek God wholeheartedly. This expressive moment in scripture should encourage you and give you confidence that it is okay to boldly affirm and declare the goodness of God. As believers we must stop using the phrase: "I match energy." As a believer, we don't match energy, we have authority to shift atmospheres. The people of Israel, by taking such an oath with loud acclamation, shouting, and the sound of trumpets and horns, were making a visible, audible, and celebratory pledge to seek the Lord with their whole hearts. Our commitment to seek God, being filled with the Spirit, can transform our personal lives and influence the world around us. We shift atmospheres by seeking the Lord wholeheartedly and allowing the Holy Spirit to fill us. Today, read Ephesians 5:18 and ask the Holy Spirit to fill you as you spend time with Him today. How do you shift the atmosphere?

We shift atmospheres by taking an oath to the Lord with loud acclamation. "Acclamation" suggest a vocal expression of approval or agreement. Come into agreement with the word of God. When you tell God who He is, He will turn around and tell you who you are. Shift the atmosphere in your relationships and friendships. Shift the atmosphere in your marriage. Shift the atmosphere in your school. Shift the atmosphere on your job.Shift the atmosphere while you are driving in your car. When you say 'yes' to stop matching energy you being to shift atmospheres for the Kingdom. Be an atmosphere changer today.

The Lord is
saying today:

Morning
Scripture

Priority
Scriptures

NOTES

Pray
PLAN
Prepare

NOTES

Pray

My Personal Prayer:

My Daily Decree:

Today, I DECREE...

Pray
PLAN
Prepare

FRIDAY
Day

19

PRAY   Plan   Prepare

COLOSSIANS 3:16 ESV

THE WORD IS ALWAYS WORTH IT....

I recently finished Lysa Terkeurst devotional: "You're Going to Make it." Listen, you must go order that today. But, a couple things just stuck to my bones. The first thing: " I can release back to God what I was never meant to carry." The word of God will always be worth it. Sitting with Jesus will always be worth it. We find in Colossians 3:16, the apostle Paul, under the inspiration of the Holy Spirit, declares, "Let the word of Christ dwell in you richly..." "The word of Christ" refers not only to the Scriptures but also to the living Savior of our lives. This scriptures is a call to immerse ourselves in the teachings and character of Christ.

As a believer, we are entrusted with the responsibility to share the profound truths of Christ's teachings, guiding and correcting one another with wisdom rooted in the Word. Word is Worth it because Jesus is worth it. The importance of fellowship and discipleship within the body of Christ should be a highlight of our faith. To "sing psalms and hymns and spiritual songs" emphasizes the role of worship in embedding the Word within our hearts. Through worship, we begin to release back to God what we were never meant to carry. This verse also encourages us to approach life "with thankfulness in our hearts to God." Remember that anxiety and gratitude can't coexist. Read John 1:1. The Word is always worth it .

NOTES

SATURDAY
Day

20

PRAY   Plan   Prepare

ISAIAH 40:31 ESV

YOUR YES DEMANDS YOU TO CARRY THE WEIGHT of the WAIT....

Isaiah 40:31 is a reminder of the powerful truth that those who wait on the Lord will find strength beyond measure. The verse says, "but they who wait for the Lord shall renew their strength; they shall mount up with wings like eagles: in a world driven by instant gratification and hurried pursuits, waiting is the hardest thing we will ever do on our Christian journey. In Isaiah, the challenge is to view waiting not as a passive endurance but as an opportunity to carry the weight of the wait with unwavering faith. The concept of waiting is not a passive idleness but an active trust. There must be an intentional pause, a surrender of our own timelines to embrace God's perfect timing. The weight of the wait should never be a burden. We must relinquish control and place our trust in Him. There is a promise that you can hold on to today: the promise of renewed strength. The wait is not a delay but a period of divine preparation. As we wait on the Lord, He is molding our character.He is doing a great work within us. He is giving us strength for the journey ahead. Eagles soar. Eagles are known for their strength, vision, and endurance. As we carry the weight of the wait, we are empowered to rise above challenges, gaining a divine perspective that transcends the limitations of our circumstances.The strategy of waiting allows us to walk through the various seasons of life with resilience, trusting that God's timing is perfect, and His plans are for our good. We shall run and not be weary, we shall walk and not faint. If you are feeling disheartened today by delays, find strength in the promise that those who wait on the Lord shall renew their strength but also soar to new heights with unwavering faith. Repeat after me: "As I say 'yes' to purpose today, I will have renewed strength by waiting on the Lord. As I say 'yes' to the promises of God I will soar to new heights because that is the will of God for my life."

NOTES

SUNDAY
Day
21

PRAY   Plan   Prepare

PSALM 139:23-24 ESV

YOUR YES WILL REQUIRE YOUR TRANSPARENCY FOR YOUR TRANSFORMATION

"Search me, O God, and know my heart;" Can we push pause for a moment? I want you to imagine someone searching your house right now. Clothes on the floor, dust on the tables and dishes in the sink. Without warning, someone knocks on your door and explains they must search your house. King David was a man after God's on heart, he penned the words of Psalm 139:23-24. In these verses, we witness David's transparency before the Lord, inviting God to examine his innermost being. David, invited God to come knock on his door, come into his house and do a full search. David's transparency led to his transformation into the man God called him to be.

Daily, we must ask God to come do a clean sweep of our hearts. Davids plea,"Search me, O God," reflects his deep desire for transparency before God. In Psalm 51:10, David writes, "Create in me a pure heart, O God, and renew a right spirit within me." I believe this should be our daily prayer to acknowledge our imperfections and ask the Lord to create and renew. Dive into Philippians 4:6-7 and 1 John 1:9, Philippians tells us how to confront our anxious thoughts and 1 John 1 gives us a strategy on how to become transparent so that we can transform. As we make daily decisions today, let us ask ourselves, do I harbor any offenses, doubts, unforgiveness or impurities in my heart? Like David, transparency leads to repentance. Repentance leads to transformation.

The Lord is
saying today:

Morning
Scripture

Priority
Scriptures

NOTES

Pray

PLAN

Prepare

MONDAY
Day
22

PRAY   Plan   Prepare

LUKE 1:37 NLT

FAILURE IS NOT AN OPTION WHEN IT COMES TO GOD...

Today, I need you to listen to "Firm Foundation" by Cody Carnes and Maverick City. Blast it as loud as you can, while reading this. I want you to place on a post it note in your car, on your job and in your bathroom: HE DOES NOT FAIL! Your scripture focus for today is Isaiah 55:11 and Joshua 21:45. Reflect on Daniel 3:28-29. After Daniel's friends Shadrach, Meshach and Abednego were thrown into the fiery furnace for refusing to worship the golden image, they were miraculously saved by God. He did not fail! Paul and Silas in Acts 16:25-26, were imprisoned in Philippi for preaching the gospel. They prayed and sang hymns to God. There was an earthquake, the doors flew open and chains were loosed.

He did not fail! As your chains are loosed this week, be reminded that He does not fail. He will not fail. Your failure is not final. You are not perfect. That chain of perfectionism that may be gripping your life, may it be broken in Jesus's name today. He's going to finish what He started. Maybe people haven't showed up for you. Maybe people have let you down. Maybe you gave up on yourself or feel like a failure. Please know today: Jesus is going to come through for you. Just hang on in there because as you say 'yes' to the hard things God is calling you to do:

HE
WILL
NOT
FAIL!

Pray

The Lord is
saying today:

Morning
Scripture

Priority
Scriptures

Pray
PLAN
Prepare

NOTES

NOTES

TUESDAY
Day
23

PRAY   Plan   Prepare

PROVERBS 4:23 ESV

YOUR YES NEEDS
YOU TO PREPARE
AND POSITION YOUR
HEART TO HIS
WORD and HIS WILL

Proverbs 4:23 encourages us to guard our hearts above all else, for everything we do flows from it. As we position and prepare our hearts this morning or whenever you read this; let us acknowledge and understand how we can guard our hearts effectively. Biblically, our hearts encompass our innermost being, including our thoughts, emotions, desires, and intentions. Jeremiah 17:9 reminds us that the heart is deceitful above all things and beyond cure. Guarding our hearts is paramount in aligning ourselves with God's will. Psalm 37:4, encourages us to delight ourselves in the Lord, and He will give us the desires of our hearts. Positioning ourselves for God's calling begins with surrendering our hearts to Him completely.

As we surrender, we position ourselves to walk in His purpose for our lives.Proverbs 16:9 reminds us that we can make our plans, but the Lord determines our steps. Preparing our hearts involves a intentional 'yes' to be receptive to God's leading. We must guard our hearts against distractions and influences that could lead us astray. As we position and prepare our hearts for God's calling, we must guard and maintain our focus on God. Preparing and positioning our heart requires discernment and vigilance from things that are not of God. As we say 'yes' to positioning our heart, we align our minds and lives that reflect Galatians 5:22-23. Positioning and preparing our hearts enables Him to work through us mightily.

The Lord is
saying today:

Morning
Scripture

Priority
Scriptures

NOTES

Pray
PLAN
Prepare

WEDNESDAY
Day 24

PRAY   Plan   Prepare

JAMES 4:3 ESV

THE ANSWER IS ALWAYS IN THE ROOM

If you have never seen "Bruce Almighty," please skip this page. Bruce Nolan is the main character in this movie. Bruce is granted divine powers by God and begins to use them selfishly to fulfill his own desires, rather than aligning with God's will or using the powers for greater good. As a result, Bruce's prayers and action often leads to chaos and unintened consequences. James 4:3 warns against praying with selfish motives. When we approach God with selfish desires, seeking to fulfill our own pleasures rather than aligning with God's will, our prayers become ineffective. Effective prayer begins with aligning our hearts with God's will. As we surrender our will to God's, our prayers become aligned with His purposes.

Please keep asking. Ask Him again. However, remember that we must seek His kingdom first. Matthew 6:33 is your friendly reminder today. When our prayers are centered on seeking God's kingdom and righteousness, rather than our own desires, we position ourselves to receive His blessings abundantly. The answer that you need is always in the room. James 1:6-7 allows us to have confidence that He hears and answers our prayers. We can experience the power of God as we: examine our hearts and motives in prayer, seeking His kingdom above all else, and praying with faith and confidence in His promises. As we respond today, please know your 'yes' may be in the room.

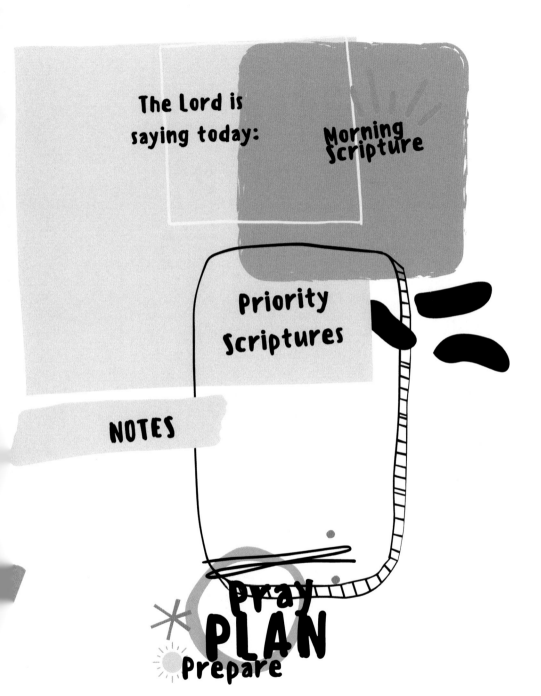

The Lord is
saying today:

Morning
Scripture

Priority
Scriptures

NOTES

Pray
PLAN
Prepare

Pray

My Personal Prayer:

My Daily Decree:

Today, I DECREE...

Pray
PLAN
Prepare

THURSDAY

Day

25

PRAY   Plan   Prepare

YOUR YES TO
GOD SHOULD
BE YOUR
GUIDING LIGHT

Faith Exercise Day:

1. Find scriptures that talk about light
2. Reflect on those scriptures and how they apply to your life
3. As you do this activity listen to: Kari Jobe- Let the Light In

The Lord is
saying today:

Morning
Scripture

Priority
Scriptures

NOTES

Pray
PLAN
Prepare

FRIDAY
Day

26

PRAY   Plan   Prepare

ISAIAH 41:10 ESV

YOUR YES WILL KEEP YOU STRONG IN EVERY STORM

Write these assurances down from God: "Do not fear, I am with you, Do not be dismayed, I will strengthen you, I will help you, I will uphold you with my righteous right hand."These words will be your strategy for your: month, your day and your season. In the Bible, numerous themes emerge, including fear, worry, and anxiety. However, amidst these themes, each mention of fear is accompanied by a story of faith that triumphs over fear's influence. As a believer, Isaiah 41:10 serves as our guiding strategy for navigating challenges and finding strength in faith. Knowing that the Lord is with us, standing beside us and living in us gives us courage to face any trial or adversity with confidence.

"Do not be dismayed." Another word for "dismayed" could be distressed or troubled. Do not be dismayed should encourage you not to be discouraged or overwhelmed by your circumstance because God is in control. There is a promise here that you and I need to stand on: "I will strengthen you." Receive that today friend. God is strengthening you even right now. "I will help you." This is a pledge from God. We don't have to tackle the issues we face alone. "I will uphold you with my righteous right hand:" this symbolizes God's power and protection. Being on the Lord side, ensures us that we are sustained and upheld by his righteousness. Your 'yes' will keep you strong in your storm.

The Lord is
saying today:

Morning
Scripture

Priority
Scriptures

NOTES

pray
PLAN
Prepare

Pray

My Personal Prayer:

My Daily Decree:
Today, I DECREE...

Pray
PLAN
Prepare

SATURDAY
Day
21

PRAY   Plan   Prepare

JOHN 13:15 ESV

IF YOU CAN POINT FINGERS YOU CAN WASH FEET

John 13:14 where Jesus sets the profound example for all of us to follow. The washing of others' feet is not only a practical act of service but also a powerful symbol of humility, servanthood, unity, forgiveness and renewal within the Christian faith. Jesus washed his disciples' feet to teach them about the importance of humility, service, and love in the kingdom of God. If you are needing a fresh touch from the Lord, humble yourself and wash feet. John 13:14-17, the humility and servant-heartedness that Jesus demonstrated by washing his disciples' feet should encourage us to serve one another with love and humility. It amazes me how many churches are in competition and conflict today. We have the audacity to say that we are believers, but point the finger before we humble ourselves to wash feet. We must remember, " If serving is below you, leadership is beyond you." Serving one another selflessly with love follows Jesus' example of sacrificial service. When was the last time you humbled yourself and washed feet? We can gossip all day, we can point the finger all day, we can fake smile for so long but until we emulate Christ's humility in our daily lives, we are doing ourselves a disservice. Like Peter, there must be a spiritual cleaning that must take place in our homes and not just the church. Jesus assures his disciples that they will be blessed if they follow his example of humility.

Humility opens the door to experiencing God's grace, peace, and abundant blessings in our lives. This week, be inspired to embrace humility in our own life. Wash your spouses feet. Ask to wash your siblings feet. If you are bold enough, have a foot washing service in your workspace. As we strive to live out the words of Jesus in John 13:14, "If I then, your Lord and Teacher, have washed your feet, you also ought to wash one another's feet." Your 'yes' needs to be a humble 'yes' this week. We have to stop being so quick to point fingers and quick enough to be humble and wash feet.

The Lord is
saying today:

Morning
Scripture

NOTES

Priority
Scriptures

Pray
PLAN
Prepare

SUNDAY
Day

28

PRAY   Plan   Prepare

YOUR YES IS A SACRED PAUSE- FIND PEACE IN THE PAUSE...

I don't know who needs to hear this, maybe it's just for me. But hear me on this day: Rest is important. I want to remind you, that rest is not only a physical necessity but also a spiritual one. You need to rest so that you can recharge. Our souls need moments of stillness to connect with God and to find renewal. Jesus often withdrew to places to pray (Luke 5:16.) Psalm 46:10 "Be still, and know I am God." Since we live in a fast-paced world, there is this pressure to constantly be productive. Find peace in the pause today! Taking time to push pause is not selfish but it is necessary for our overall health and well-being. Your marked moment of stillness will allow for an opportunity to draw close to God.

I want to encourage you over and over again, that God is present in the stillness and the silence. There is peace in your pause. As you draw closer to God, listen to His voice and experience His peace. Allow the busyness of your life to be pushed to the back burner. Read Matthew 11:28-30. Yes, you may just need a nap. But, for some of us we need to be okay with taking intentional pauses to seek God, rest and reflect. Hannah in 1 Samuel 1:9-18 found peace in the pause. David in Psalm 62:1-2 found peace in the pause. Elijah in 1 Kings 19:1-8 found peace in the pause. For 40 days and 40 nights fasting and seeking God's guidance, Moses in Exodus 24:18; Exodus 34:28 found peace in the pause. You, too can find peace in the pause.

NOTES

Pray

My Personal Prayer:

My Daily Decree:
Today, I DECREE...

Pray
PLAN
Prepare

MONDAY
Day

29

PRAY   Plan   Prepare

LUKE 17:6 ESV
EMBRACING
UNCOMMON
TERRITORY
WITH
MUSTARD
SEED FAITH

Faith Exercise Day! Push pause today. In your journal or in this blank space, write down the first things that come to your mind. Also, take at least three minutes to sit in complete silence. Silence your thoughts. After your silent meditation, ask Holy Spirit to download wisdom and knowledge. He will meet you in the pause.

Play a worship set to set the atmosphere. I suggest: Instrumental. But, whatever pushes you in the presence. Bible journal through Luke 11 while listening to the voice of God.

The Lord is
saying today:

Morning
Scripture

NOTES

Priority
Scriptures

Pray
PLAN
Prepare

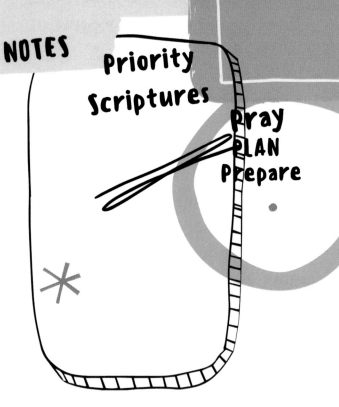

TUESDAY
Day
30

PRAY   Plan   Prepare

EXODUS 4:10-14 ESV

DEVOTED TO MY YES, NO MORE EXCUSES

Faith exercise day!
In the space provided: On the left side,
write down all of the excuses you have
ever used to get out of something God
told you do.

On the right side: If you said YES
to everything God told you to do
(just today,) what would that
unlock in your life?

The Lord is
saying today:

Morning
Scripture

NOTES

Priority
Scriptures

Pray
PLAN
Prepare

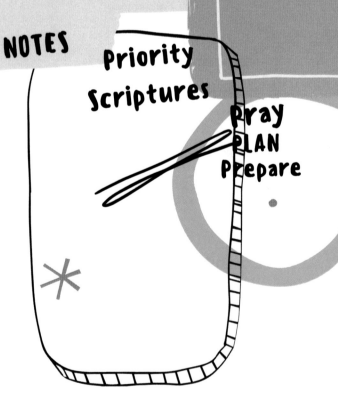

WEDNESDAY
Day 31

PRAY   Plan   Prepare

MATTHEW 10:16 ESV

I'VE GOT 99
PROBLEMS
BUT MY
FAITH AIN'T
ONE

Your problems will not trump the promises of God. In Matthew 10:16, Jesus instructs his disciples to be wise and innocent. As you read Matthew 10:16 today, write down some key words that may stick out to you. What does it mean to you to be wise as serpents and innocent as doves? Seeking wisdom may look different for everyone. James 1:5 ESV "If any of you lacks wisdom, let him ask God, who gives generously to all without reproach, and it will be given him." You and I, must posture ourselves to seek wisdom through prayer and study. How can we have 99 problems and not seek the face of the Lord? Through prayer, we align our hearts with God's will and invite His guidance into our circumstances. That's the theme of this devotional.

Saying 'YES' to God invites His guidance, His counsel, His word, His thoughts into our circumstances. If we can carve out a time to study scripture, the word will then equip us with the knowledge and discernment necessary to make wise decisions. I was a little offended when the word called me a serpent. I was like, "now wait a minute Jesus!" But, just as a serpent carefully calculates its movements, we must approach life's challenges with strategic insight, relying on the wisdom imparted by our Heavenly Father. You may have 99 problems, but your faith can't be the problem. We are called to persevere in faith.

Now, like doves, which symbolizes peace and purity, we can maintain an unwavering trust in promises amidst the storms of life. We must cultivate a spirit of resilience. Again, you are not meant to face challenges alone. Even Jesus sent his disciples out two by two. Your community matters. Your village matters. We must remain steadfast in our faith. The promises of God will always prevail over our problems. Your 'YES' may cause 99 problems, but your faith will remain. Your hope should endure. Your love should persist.

NOTES

THURSDAY
Day
32

PRAY   Plan   Prepare

YOUR YES IN DISTRESS: EMBRACING THE HANNAH ANOINTING

Hannah, in 1 Samuel 1:15-16, who was barren and deeply distressed, pours out her heart to God in prayer. When was the last time you poured out your soul to the Lord? How can one embrace the "Hannah anointing?" The first strategy, praying fervently. Fervent prayer involves a surrender of one's heart. Fervent prayer can also look like demonstrating a strong desire for God's intervention or guidance in your situation. Fervent prayer means you are blocking out distractions to commune deeply with Him. Fervent prayer may involve making requests to God but, fervent prayer invites a willingness to submit to His sovereign will, wisdom and His timing. The "Hannah anointing" demands a fervent prayer lifestyle.

Hannah finds herself in a desperate situation. She expresses her deepest needs, desires and hopes before Him. She sought the Lord, and He heard and He answered! Hannah surrendered her desire for a Child to God. She recognized that God's timing was perfect. She surrounded herself with wise counsel and she remained being faithful in a faithless circumstance. You can receive the "Hannah anointing" by surrendering your own desires, trusting in His timing, surrounding yourself with a wise and encouraging community. Lastly, you and I must remain faithful. It's okay to pray passionately and sincerely in your grief, your hurt, your joy, your sorrow. The Lord wants to hear from you.

NOTES

Pray

My Personal Prayer:

My Daily Decree:
Today, I DECREE...

Pray
PLAN
Prepare

FRIDAY

Day

33

PRAY   Plan   Prepare

MATTHEW 11:1 ESV

The Divine Patterns of 12 and 3

Matthew 17:1: Peter, James and John were led up a high mountain by themselves. Although there were twelve disciples there were only three that were able to go up higher. The Lord really highlighted twelve and three to me in the past month. In the Bible, the number 12 is often associated with completeness, governance, and divine order. We see this reflected in the twelve tribes of Israel and the twelve apostles chosen by Jesus.These twelve disciples were handpicked by Jesus to accompany Him, learn from Him, and carry on His mission after His departure. Despite the multitude of followers, Jesus selected only three— Peter, James, and John—to accompany Him on significant occasions such as the transfiguration and His agony in the garden of Gethsemane. Midnight and 3 PM hold special significance in Scripture, representing moments of divine intervention and revelation. Midnight symbolizes the darkness of sin and the need for redemption, while 3 PM marks the hour of Jesus' death on the cross, the moment when the veil in the temple was torn, granting access to God's presence for all believers. These two moments serve as bookends to the pivotal events of Jesus' crucifixion and resurrection, demonstrating God's power to conquer sin and death.The number 3 is often associated with divine perfection and completeness in the Bible. It represents the Trinity—Father, Son, and Holy Spirit—three persons in one God. As disciples, let us reflect today on His sovereignty. His completeness. His faithfulness to us.

Your 'yes' needs to recognize divine patterns and rhythms of God. Jesus used parables. Matthew 13:1-23; Luke 10:25-37. Parables are significant patterns to reveal truths about the Kingdom of God. Miracles on Miracles are patterns of God. Jesus performed numerous of miracles throughout the word of God. Miracles are the demonstration of His divine authority. Another divine pattern is prayer. Jesus often withdrew to pray alone, particularly before significant events or decisions. Your 'yes' needs you to recognize divine patterns and apply them to your life. Divine patterns can reflect the rhythm and structures of Christ's ministry and teaching. If you want to experience the power of Christ you must understand the patterns of God.

SATURDAY
Day 34

PRAY   Plan   Prepare

Touching the Hem touched Him

Yesterday, we talked about the divine pattern of twelve and three. Here, in Matthew 9:20-25 we find a woman whose name is not known, but her issue was. This woman suffered from a bleeding disorder for twelve years. She dared to reach out in faith to touch the hem of Jesus and experienced a miraculous healing. I want to encourage you today that you are not your issue. Your 'yes' to touch His hem will allow you to touch Him. Throughout this devotion, my prayer has been,"Lord make us desperate to say yes to your word and your will." I also want to encourage you that your condition is never beyond the healing power of Jesus. Do you have desperate faith? Are you desperate for a divine encounter?

Today, I pray that you approach the throne of grace with confidence, trusting in God's power to be healed and restored. Your 'yes' will require a desperate faith. What does desperate faith look like? It looks like: dying to self. It looks like: not people pleasing. Desperate faith is being in a crowd of people that may not know your name but know your issue and relentlessly pursuing to touch a small part of his hem. It's making a sacrificial 'yes' of fasting and praying even when you don't feel like it. Once you touch Him your issues change. Your heart changes. Most importantly your name changes. You are no longer your issue. Your 'Yes' allows you to find your identity in Him. I want to encourage you to His hem today.

The Lord is
saying today:

NOTES

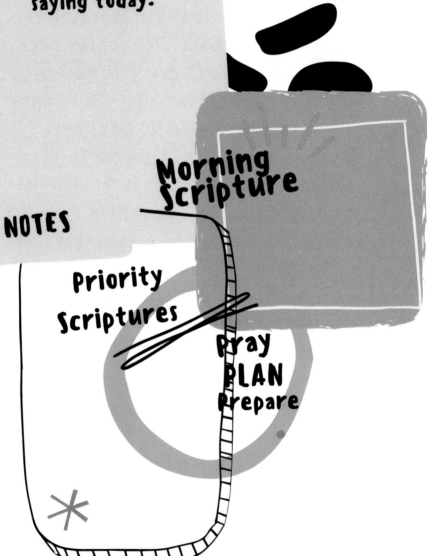

Morning
Scripture

Priority
Scriptures

Pray
PLAN
Prepare

Pray

My Personal Prayer:

My Daily Decree:
Today, I DECREE...

Pray
PLAN
Prepare

SUNDAY
Day

35

PRAY   Plan   Prepare

Philippians 4:8 ESV

Your Yes will demand you to be allergic to avearage

"Finally, brothers, whatever is true, what is honorable, whatever is just, whatever is pure, whatever is lovely, whatever is commendable, if there is any excellence, if there is anything worth of praise, think about these things." At this point in your life, what you are going to read next, may not be for you. Going above and beyond in all aspects of life may exhaust you. Even the thought of rejecting mediocrity and embracing a higher standard of moral conduct, spiritual growth and service to others may not make your heart race anymore. That's okay. Friend, I believe, we can get stagnant in our walk with Christ. I do believe that we can do just a little to make it "look" like we are serving. I do believe we can settle for mediocrity, when the Lord is calling us to not settle for average. Be allergic to average.

Serving goes beyond the four walls of your church. Being allergic to average can look like different things for different people. Philippians 4:8 says: whatever is true, whatever is noble, right, pure, lovely.. it then goes on to say: whatever is excellent. Anything reflecting goodness deserves admiration and praise. Today, I want you to think of the song "Goodness of God." "His goodness is running after, it's running after me." Jesus wants the best for you. He is the best thing that Has ever happened to you. But, settling for this mediocre approach and having this average mindset can no longer be in your heart. How can you become allergic to average when it comes to your walk with Christ? Reflect tonight on what you have settled for instead of going after the excellencies of Christ.

NOTES

MONDAY
Day
36

PRAY   Plan   Prepare

2 CORINTHIANS 9:6-7 ESV

DESTINY DEPOSITS